This Bible belongs to

_____

_____

This book tells how God made
wonderful promises to his people
– and how he kept those promises.

Beginning with God's promise to give
Abram and his family a land of their own,
we follow the adventures of the people
of Israel in good times and bad.

Until God sent a very special person –
Jesus – to save the world.
Just as he promised!

Copyright © 2016 Lion Hudson/
Tim Dowley Associates Ltd
Illustrations copyright © 2003 Eira Reeves

The right of Eira Reeves to be identified as
the author and illustrator of this work has
been asserted by her in accordance with the
Copyright, Designs and Patents Acts 1988.

All rights reserved.

Published by Candle Books
an imprint of
Lion Hudson plc
Wilkinson House, Jordan Hill Road,
Oxford OX2 8DR, England
www.lionhudson.com/candle

ISBN 978 1 78128 264 9
e-ISBN 978 1 78128 293 9

First edition 2016

The Lord's Prayer (on page 96) is adapted
from the Good News Bible © 1994 published
by the Bible Societies/HarperCollins
Publishers Ltd UK, Good News Bible ©
American Bible Society 1966, 1971, 1976,
1992. Used with permission.

A catalogue record for this book
is available from the British Library

Printed and bound in Malaysia,
January 2016, LH18

Would you like to know?
Bible
Storybook

written and illustrated
by Eira Reeves

CANDLE
BOOKS

Old Testament

New Testament

Abram leaves home

Long, long ago, in a far-off land called Ur,
there lived a man named Abram.
One day God spoke to him.

"I am going to give you a special land,"
God promised. "Look up! Can you count
the stars? One day there will be more people
in your family than there are stars in the sky!"

So Abram packed his bags and loaded up his animals. Then he set out with his family to look for this special land.
He believed God.

After many months, Abram came at last to
the land God had promised. There he stayed
with his wife, Sarah, and their son, Isaac.

Genesis 12:1–9, 21:1–7

God changed Abram's name to Abraham.
And God gave Abraham great flocks of sheep
and herds of camels.

Now Abraham's son, Isaac, had two sons,
Esau and Jacob. Esau was a hunter, but Jacob,
the younger son, was very sneaky.

One day, Jacob went to his blind, old father,
and pretended to be Esau.
Isaac gave Jacob his special blessing,
instead of Esau.

Esau was so angry, that Jacob had to run away.
He went to a far country.

Genesis 25:19–34, 27:1–45

15

One night, as Jacob slept on a rock,
he dreamed he saw angels climbing
up and down stairs to heaven.
God promised him,
"I will always look after
your family."

Genesis 28:10–22

Years later, Jacob came back
to the Promised Land.
Jacob made up with his brother, Esau.
Now Jacob had a big family of twelve sons.

Jacob loved Joseph more than
his older brothers.
Jacob gave him a special coat.
How wonderful he looked!

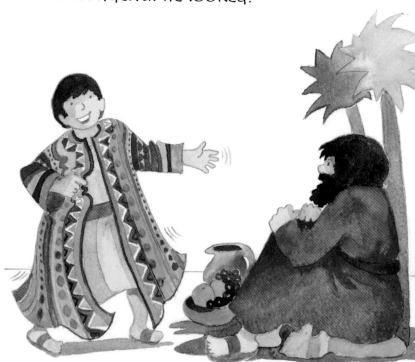

And how jealous Joseph's brothers were!
They were so angry that they took Joseph
and sold him to traders.
They told Jacob that Joseph was dead.
Jacob wept.

Genesis 37:1–36

Joseph had lots of adventures in Egypt.
First he was an army captain's slave,
then he was thrown into jail.
Finally Joseph was made top minister
to Pharaoh, the ruler of Egypt!

Genesis 38–41

One year, no rain fell.
No one could find enough to eat.
But in Egypt, Joseph had saved grain
in huge barns.

When Jacob heard this, he took his family
to Egypt to get food.
How glad he was to find his son Joseph alive!

Genesis 42–47

Escape to freedom!

So Joseph's family settled in Egypt.
They were called "Hebrews"
– and kept growing in number.
Years later, a new pharaoh
made the Hebrews work as slaves.

He was scared that there
were too many Hebrews.
"Kill every Hebrew baby boy!"
he ordered.

But one Hebrew mother hid her baby,
named Moses, in a basket.
Pharaoh's daughter, the princess of Egypt,
found the basket floating in the river.
Moses was safe!

Exodus 2:1–11

So the princess took the young boy
to her palace.
He was brought up as a royal prince.

When Moses grew up,
he ran away from Egypt
and went to live in the desert.
One day, an angel spoke to him
from a burning bush.
"Go and tell Pharaoh,
'Let my people go!'"

Exodus 3

Moses was scared.
But he went to Pharaoh
many times, saying,
"Let my people go!"
At last Pharaoh gave in.
"Go – and take all
your people with you!"

Exodus 10:21–29

Quickly, the Hebrews prepared to leave.
They set out for the land that God
had promised them.

Exodus 12:31–39

Pharaoh chased after the Hebrews.
But when he came to the Red Sea,
Pharaoh and all his soldiers drowned.
God saved Moses and his people!

Exodus 14

The Hebrews stayed in the desert
for many years.
God gave them special food called manna.
But they often grumbled and moaned.
They even made a gold statue
and danced around it!

Exodus 16, 32

One day, Moses climbed a high mountain.
He came down carrying two great stones.
On them were God's
rules for everyone.
We call them the
Ten Commandments.

Exodus 20

God told his people to build a really big tent,
where the priests could pray to God.
When they moved on, they folded up the
tent and took it with them.

Exodus 26

Into the Promised Land

As they got nearer to the Promised Land,
Moses sent spies to explore.
Two came back saying,
"It's a land full of fruit and good food."

Numbers 13

After many years, Moses died.
God's people crossed the River Jordan.
They entered the Promised Land
– but they still had to capture it.

Joshua 3–4

God gave special orders for attacking
the city of Jericho.
The people walked around and around it.
When the trumpets blew and the people
shouted, the walls fell down!

Joshua 5:13 – 6:27

God gave his people new leaders.
One great leader was named Gideon.

Judges 6

With God's help, Gideon beat Israel's enemies.
He attacked at night, with flaming torches
and lots of noise!
The enemy ran away terrified.

Judges 7

At harvest time, the people had
a great festival.
They thanked God for all the fruits
and grain in the Promised Land.

Leviticus 23

But the people were not happy.
"Give us a king!" they demanded.
"Everyone else has a king."

1 Samuel 8

Kings and prophets

So God told his prophet, Samuel,
where to find a man fit to be
king of Israel.
His name was Saul.

Samuel poured oil on Saul's head.
This showed everyone that
God had chosen him
to become king.

1 Samuel 9–10

At first Saul ruled well.
He led his army against
many enemies.

1 Samuel 14:15–23

But later Saul disobeyed God.
So God sent Samuel
to find a new king.

1 Samuel 15

Samuel found a boy looking
after his father's sheep.
His name was David.
Samuel knew that God had chosen him
to become the next king of Israel.

David was very bold.
He killed the giant Goliath
with his sling.
The people sang,
"How brave David is!"

1 Samuel 17

David became a great king.
He loved to play his harp
and sing of God's love.

David made Jerusalem his chief city.

2 Samuel 5

David brought the special holy box
that contained the Ten Commandments
to Jerusalem.
He sang and danced in front of it.

2 Samuel 6

When David died, his son
Solomon became king.
Solomon was very wise.

1 Kings 2

When people had problems,
they came to Solomon
to ask him what they should do.

1 Kings 3

The queen of Sheba lived far away.
She journeyed for days to hear
Solomon's wise words.

1 Kings 10:1–13

King Solomon built a beautiful
new temple in Jerusalem.
It was made of the best gold,
wood, and stone.

1 Kings 6

The people disobey God

After Solomon died, the people
disobeyed God's laws.
The kingdom was split in two:
one part was called Judah,
the other Israel.

God sent special messengers called prophets.
They told the people to return to God's way.
The prophet Elijah warned wicked King Ahab.

"Worship the living God," said Elijah.
When he prayed, God sent down
fire from heaven.

1 Kings 17–18

60

The prophet Jeremiah warned that there would be war if the people did not turn back to God.

God sent many other prophets.
He sent Isaiah, Daniel, Jonah,
and a shepherd named Amos.

They warned the Israelites,
"Mend your ways
– or God will send
enemies to
defeat you."

But still the people didn't listen
So cruel kings came and took
the Israelites away to be slaves
They burned the beautiful
city of Jerusalem.

2 Kings 2?

But the prophets had words of hope, too.
"God still loves you," they said.
"He will send a special person,"
promised the prophets.
"He will save us."

Many years later that special
person came, just as God promised.
His name was Jesus.

Luke 4:14–21

The story of Jesus

Prophets said that a special baby would be born in the little town of Bethlehem.

Isaiah 7:14

He would be called
the Prince of Peace.

This map shows the land where Jesus lived.

The first Christmas

In a town called Nazareth there lived a young woman named Mary.

One day an angel appeared to Mary.
"You are going to give birth to a
very special baby," he said.
"You must call
the baby Jesus."

Luke 1:26–38

Mary went to tell her cousin Elizabeth.
Elizabeth was expecting a baby too.
His name was to be John.
Both women were overjoyed.

Luke 1:39–45

Soon Mary married a carpenter named Joseph.
They had to make a long journey to Bethlehem.
Mary was very tired when they arrived.

Luke 2:1–7

They could find nowhere to sleep.

An innkeeper said,
"You can stay in my stable."
Mary and Joseph accepted gladly.

That night some shepherds were
sleeping in fields near Bethlehem.

Suddenly they saw a bright light.
An angel appeared and said,
"Tonight a child is born in Bethlehem.
He has come to save his people."

The shepherds rushed off at once
to find the newborn baby.

Luke 2:8–20

Far away, some wise men
saw a special, new star in the sky.
They decided to follow the star
to find the newborn baby.

They took with them precious gifts:
gold, frankincense, and myrrh.

At last the wise men came
to the little town of Bethlehem,
where the star shone down.

When they saw baby Jesus,
they knelt down to worship him.

Matthew 2:1–12

Jesus grows up

Mary and Joseph took Jesus back
to their home in Nazareth.

Here Jesus grew up.
He helped his parents
and played with his friends.

Matthew 2:19–23

When Jesus was twelve, he went to Jerusalem
with his parents for a special holiday.
But Mary and Joseph lost him in the crowds.

At last they found Jesus again.
He was talking to the Jewish
lawyers in the Temple.
They were astonished at the
wise things young Jesus said.

Luke 2:41–52

When Jesus grew up,
he worked with Joseph
as a carpenter.
But he knew God
had a special job
for him to do.

Jesus' special work

Jesus' cousin, John, started to preach beside the River Jordan.

He told people to turn away from the bad things they were doing.

He dipped them into the river to show
they were making a clean start.

Matthew 3:1–12

Jesus came to the river and
asked John to baptize him.
As Jesus was baptized,
the Holy Spirit came
down like a dove.

This was the beginning
of Jesus' special work,
the work that God
wanted him to do.

Luke 3:1–22

Jesus went to Lake Galilee.
He called twelve men as his special followers:
Simon Peter and his brother Andrew;
James and his brother John;

Philip, Bartholomew, Matthew the tax-man, Thomas the twin, another James, Simon, Judas, and Judas Iscariot.

Mark 1:14–20, 3:13–19

Jesus taught his disciples how to pray:

Our Father in heaven:
Holy is your name;
May your kingdom come;
May your will be done
here on earth
just as it is in heaven.
Give us today
the food we need.
Forgive us the wrongs
we have done,
as we forgive those
who have wronged us.
Do not bring us
to hard testing,
but keep us safe
from evil.
Amen.

Matthew 6:9–15

Jesus began to travel to nearby
towns and villages.

He told people special stories
about how God wants our world to be.
People were amazed when they
heard him speak.

Jesus loved children.
He said we should never harm them.

Luke 18:15–17

He wanted people to
love one another.
Jesus said:
"You should
always forgive
each other."

Luke 17:3–4

Many sick people came to Jesus.
People with bad backs and bad legs.
People who couldn't see and couldn't hear.

Jesus healed them all.

Jesus often did special miracles.
One day he fed 5,000 people
with just five loaves and two fish!

Luke 9:10–17

Jesus goes to Jerusalem

Jesus loved Jerusalem.
It was a beautiful city.

He decided to travel there again.
Jesus told his disciples,
"I am soon going to die."
They didn't understand.

Luke 18:31–34

Some of the people in Jerusalem hated Jesus.
"He doesn't keep our laws," they said.
So they plotted against him.

Judas, one of Jesus' own followers,
turned against him.
He made a plot with Jesus' enemies.

Luke 22:1–6

Jesus arrived in Jerusalem at festival time.
He borrowed a donkey to ride into the city.

When the people saw him coming,
they waved palm branches.
"Jesus is our king!" they shouted.

Luke 19:28–38

One night Jesus ate a special supper
with his disciples.
Again he said, "I'm going to die soon."
They didn't understand why he said this.

Jesus broke bread and poured wine.
"Every time you eat bread or drink wine,"
he said, "remember me."

Luke 22:14–20

Then Jesus and his disciples
went out to a garden.
Jesus prayed to his heavenly Father.
The disciples fell asleep.

Luke 22:39–46

The first Easter

While they were in the garden, Judas brought Jesus' enemies to arrest him. Jesus' disciples ran away.

Soldiers took Jesus to the Roman ruler.
He said, "This man has done nothing wrong!"

But the people shouted,
"Kill Jesus! Kill him!"

Luke 22:47–53, 22:66 – 23:25

So soldiers took Jesus away.
They put him to death
on a wooden cross.

Luke 23:26–46

Jesus' friends were very sad.
They had lost a special person.

They put Jesus' body in a cave
and rolled a huge stone across the doorway.

Luke 23:50–56

When some friends went back to the tomb,
they saw two angels inside.
"Don't be afraid!" said the angels.
"Jesus is alive! Go and meet him in Galilee."

Jesus is alive!

Next Peter and John ran to Jesus' tomb.
They saw that the stone was rolled away.
They were astonished!

John 20:1–9

Soon afterwards, the disciples went fishing.
They saw Jesus on the beach.

Peter was so pleased to see Jesus again
that he jumped into the water
and rushed ashore.

John 21:1–14

Not long after this, Jesus left them.
He returned to his heavenly Father.
But the disciples knew he was alive forever.

Luke 24:50–53

And Jesus promised:
"One day I will return as king!"